# ILLUSTRATED BIBLE STORIES

MARION THOMAS AND DANIELE FABBRI

# Contents

# A WONDERFUL CREATION

*Genesis 1:1-31*

In the beginning there was nothing at all. Only God was there.

God spoke, and then there was light in the darkness.

God created snow-topped mountains and deep blue seas.

God covered the land with tall trees and scented flowers.

God made the spinning earth, the red hot sun and the silvery moon. God scattered stars across space.

God filled the sea with fish and the sky with birds, bees and

butterflies. God created animals that crawled on the land. God
made people like himself: caring, thinking, feeling, able to love
and to be loved.

God was pleased with everything he had made. It was very
good.

# Adam and Eve choose

*Genesis 3:1-24*

Adam and Eve lived and worked in the Garden of Eden and they were happy.

God asked them to choose names for the creatures he had created and to take care of them. The garden was full of delicious fruits and vegetables, and they could eat anything they wanted, except from one tree.

'Eat and enjoy the fruit of all the trees except the one in the middle of the garden. If you eat from the tree of the knowledge of good and evil, you will die,' said God.

One day the serpent crept up to Eve and whispered in her ear.

'Did God tell you not to eat from this tree? Look how good the fruit looks. You won't die if you eat this fruit. You will know everything. You will be like God himself.'

Eve looked at the tree. The fruit looked delicious. She took a big, deep bite. Then she gave some to Adam.

Suddenly Adam and Eve knew what they had done. They didn't feel the same any more. They had disobeyed God. They knew how it felt to betray someone and to feel guilt, and they hid from God, their creator, their friend.

God made them clothes to wear from animal skins and sent them away from the beautiful garden.

# Noah's Ark

*Genesis 6:9 – 7:10*

Noah loved God. But the people around him lied and cheated; they hurt and killed one another. They forgot all about the God who had made them.

'I am going to flood the earth with water, and wash it clean,' God said to Noah.

God gave Noah careful instructions about how to build a huge ark. It had to be large enough to protect Noah, his family and all the different kinds of animals. Noah cut down trees, hammered in nails and made the boat just as God had told him. Then he covered the ark with thick, sticky tar to keep the water out. People watched and wondered, but they all thought Noah was mad to be building an ark.

When it was finished, The creatures came to NOAH, male and female of every kind of bird and animal, and Noah found room for them on his ark.

Then it began to rain. Noah, his family and all the animals were safe inside the ark.

For forty day and forty nights, the rain came down and flooded the earth.

# THE FLOOD AND THE RAINBOW

*Genesis 7:11 – 9:17*

When the rain stopped falling, the ark floated on the flood waters.

After some time the waters began to go down and the ark came to rest on a mountain top.

When the earth was dry again, God told Noah to open the door. The animals ran free and made their homes on the new land.

Noah thanked God for keeping them safe from the flood and watched as a bright rainbow coloured the sky.

'When you look at the rainbow,' said
God, 'it will remind you of my promise that
I will never destroy the earth by flood again.'

# THE FATHER OF A NATION

*Genesis 12:1-3*

Abraham lived in the city of Ur. One day God spoke to Abraham.

'I want you to move from here and go to live in the land I will give you,' God said. 'I will show you where to go and will provide you with a new home. I will bless you, and your family will be the start of a great nation.'

'We must pack up our things,' Abraham told Sarah, his wife. 'We must go to the place where God leads us.'

So Abraham and Sarah began their journey, with their servants and their camels, their sheep and their goats.

They walked by day and each night they stopped and camped in their tents. They did not know where they were going, but Abraham knew that God had promised to be with them wherever they went.

At the end of a long, long journey, they reached the land of Canaan.

'This is the land that I will give to you and your children,' said God. 'It is a beautiful land where you can graze your animals and have all that you need.'

Abraham thanked God and rested from his journey. He put up his tent to make his home in the land God had promised to give him.

# ABRAHAM TRUSTS GOD

*Genesis 15:1-6*

Abraham and Sarah had no children. Now they were old and Abraham wondered how he could be the start of a new nation without a child.

'I will look after you,' God promised. 'I will give you everything you need!'

'But Lord God,' said Abraham, 'what I really want is a baby boy.'

'I promise you will have a son of your own,' said God. 'Look up at the sky, Abraham.'

Abraham looked up. The sky was full of stars, twinkling in the darkness.

'Can you count the stars?' asked God.

Abraham shook his head.

'One day there will be as many people in your family as the number of stars in the sky!' said God.

Abraham trusted God to keep his promise. Some time later, Sarah found she was expecting a baby. She gave birth to a lovely baby boy. They called him Isaac.

Isaac was a very special baby. Through him, God would give Abraham grandchildren and great grandchildren, and give those grandchildren great grandchildren of their own: the start of a new nation.

# JACOB'S FAVOURITE SON

*Genesis 37:3-28*

Abraham's grandson, Jacob had a great big family. But he loved Joseph best of all. Jacob gave Joseph a beautiful coloured coat to wear. Joseph liked to show it off to everyone.

Joseph's big brothers saw how much their father loved Joseph. They were jealous of him.

One day, Joseph's big brothers were taking care of their father's sheep.

'Here comes Joseph!' groaned one of them.

'Let's kill him!' said another. 'No one will know. We could say he's been eaten by a wild animal!'

'No, don't kill him,' said Reuben. 'Put him in this empty well.'

His brothers grabbed him, tore off his beautiful coat, and threw him down into the well.

Soon some traders passed by on their way to Egypt.

'Let's sell Joseph,' the brothers decided. 'Let him see how he likes being a slave in Egypt.'

But God had plans for Joseph. Even in Egypt, God was looking after him.

# PHARAOH'S DREAMS



Joseph was the slave of a man named Potiphar. But Potiphar's wife told lies about him – and Joseph found himself behind bars in Pharaoh's prison.

One day the king of Egypt had his baker and his wine-taster thrown into the prison. Both the men had strange dreams. With God's help, Joseph explained that the wine-taster would get back his job but the baker would be executed. It all happened just as Joseph said.

Two years later, the king of Egypt had strange dreams. The wine-taster remembered Joseph.

The king explained his dreams about seven fat cows being swallowed up by seven thin, bony cows and seven ripe ears of corn being swallowed up by seven thin, sun-scorched ears of corn.

'God is sending you a warning,' explained Joseph. 'Seven years of good harvests will be followed by seven years of famine. Store up food in the years of plenty so that the people can eat when the harvests fail.'

The king of Egypt gave Joseph the job of making sure there was food for everyone. Joseph became the most important man in Egypt.

When the famine came, Joseph was there to help not just the Egyptians, but his whole family who came to live with him in Egypt.

# THE BABY IN THE BASKET

*Exodus 2:1-10*

By the time Joseph died Egypt was full of God's people. Pharaohs came and went until no one remembered Joseph at all.

Then a new Pharaoh made God's people slaves. He worked the people hard, afraid they would rebel against him. Then he decided to kill all their baby boys.

When Jochebed's baby son was born, she hid him. But as he grew, he made more noise. She was afraid the soldiers would find him.

His big sister Miriam watched her mother weave a basket and cover it with tar. She went with her as she hid it on the bank of the River Nile with her little brother inside it. Then Miriam hid too.

Pharaoh's daughter saw the basket. She lifted the lid to see a little baby boy crying.

'You are one of the Israelite babies,' she said gently. 'Don't cry.'

Miriam came out and offered to bring her mother to nurse the baby.

'I will call the baby Moses,'

the princess said to Jochebed. 'Look after him. When he is old enough, he can live with me at the palace.'

TROUBLE IN EGYPT
Exodus 6:28 – 12:31

Moses knew that the Egyptians
treated God's people badly. Now he was a
man, God wanted Moses to speak to the
king.

'Tell Pharaoh to let my people go!' God
said.

Moses was afraid. He didn't want to go.
But he went with his brother Aaron.

The king listened; but he did not
know the God of Moses and Aaron; and
he needed his slaves. He refused to let
the people go.

So God sent plagues on Egypt.
First, all the water in the Nile
turned to blood; then there were
frogs, gnats and flies; the cattle
died and the people came out
in spots; hail fell like stones
from the sky; and the crops
were eaten by locusts. Then
an inky darkness covered
Egypt. Finally, the eldest
child in every family died.

'Take your people
and go!' said Pharaoh.

# CROSSING THE RED SEA

*Exodus 14:5-31*

The Israelites had not gone far when the king of Egypt sent chariots to make them return.

The Israelites had reached the shores of the Red Sea when they saw they were trapped, with the Egyptians behind them and the sea in front of them.

'Don't be afraid,' Moses told the people. 'God will save us.'

Moses stretched out his hand across the sea. A strong wind stirred up the waters until a path appeared so the Israelites could walk across on dry land. When the Egyptians tried to follow, the waters returned. God's people were safe on the other side.

Now they were free to love God and follow his ways. God led them home through the desert to the land of Canaan.

DAVID AND THE KING
1 Samuel 16:14 – 17:40

David was the youngest of eight brothers. The three eldest were soldiers in King Saul's army. David was King Saul's armour bearer. He played the harp for him when he became depressed.

When he was not with the king, David looked after his father's sheep in the hills around Bethlehem. Sometimes he killed lions or bears with a stone thrown from his sling. David trusted God to look after him.

One day, David's father sent him to see his brothers. As he walked among the soldiers, David saw that they were very frightened. Goliath, the Philistines' champion soldier, was challenging them to fight – and Goliath was huge.

'Who will come and fight me?' the giant shouted.

No one stepped forward. No one wanted to fight Goliath, except David.

King Saul offered David his armour, but it was too big for him. He offered David his sword, but it was too heavy.

# DAVID AND THE GIANT

*1 Samuel 17:41-51*

David picked up five smooth stones from the stream and went out with his sling to fight the giant.

When Goliath saw that the Israelites had sent a boy to fight him, he was angry.

'You have a sharp sword,' shouted David. 'But I have the living God on my side! Soon everyone will know that there is a God in Israel.'

David put a stone in his sling, whirled it around his head, and aimed it at Goliath. Then David watched as the giant fell heavily to the ground.

The Philistines turned and ran. The Israelite army cheered. David was right. God really was on their side!

# Jonah Runs Away



'Tell the people in Nineveh to stop doing evil things,' God said to the prophet Jonah.

But Jonah didn't want to go to Nineveh. Instead he boarded a ship going in the opposite direction.

Then a fierce storm blew up.

'Pray to your God or we will all die!' they shouted at Jonah.

'Throw me overboard!' Jonah said. 'This is all my fault.'

As soon as the sailors threw Jonah into the sea, the wind dropped and the sea was calm. A huge fish came and swallowed Jonah up whole. He sat inside the belly of the fish for three days and nights and prayed.

'I'm sorry, Lord!' he prayed. 'I should have done what you asked me to do.'

Then God caused the big fish to spit Jonah out on to dry land.

Jonah went to Nineveh and told them that God loved them and they should stop doing wicked things. The people of Nineveh were sorry. They stopped their evil ways. And God forgave them.

# DANIEL IS THROWN TO THE LIONS

*Daniel 6:1-23*

Daniel lived in the land of Babylon.
He had been taken from his home far away
and made to work for King Darius.

Daniel loved God and prayed to
him three times a day. The king saw that he
was honest and hard working and gave him an
important job in his kingdom. But there were
men in Babylon who wanted to make trouble for
Daniel.

'You are such a great king!' they said to King
Darius. 'You should make a new law so that no one
should worship anyone but you. Anyone who breaks
this law must be thrown into a den of lions!'

The king made the law. But Daniel worshipped
God as usual and prayed three times a day.

The men knew Daniel loved God more than his
life. Now Daniel had to be taken to the den of lions
and left there to die.

The next morning the king went to the lions'
den.

'Daniel!' he shouted. 'Has your God been able
to save you from the lions' teeth?'

'I am here, my King!' replied Daniel. 'God has
kept me safe.'

Then King Darius made a new law.

'From now on,' he said, 'everyone must worship
Daniel's God, the true and living God!'

# MARY'S BABY BOY

*Luke 2:1-20*

Mary was engaged to be married to Joseph, who was a carpenter in Nazareth. One day the angel Gabriel came to Mary.

'Don't be afraid,' he said. 'God is very pleased with you. You will have a baby, God's only Son, and you will call him Jesus. He will bring peace to the world!'

'I want to do whatever God wants,' Mary answered.

Some time later Mary and Joseph travelled to Bethlehem to be counted by the Romans.

Bethlehem was bustling with people and there was no room in the inn. Mary knew that her baby would soon be born. When the innkeeper offered them his stable, she was pleased to have somewhere to rest.

That night, Mary gave birth to a baby boy. She wrapped him in strips of cloth and made a bed for him in a manger.

During the night, shepherds came to see Mary's baby. Angels told them that Jesus, the Saviour of the world, had been born in Bethlehem.

# Travellers from the East

*Matthew 2:1-12*

Far away, in another country, wise men saw a new star in the sky.

'It means a new king has been born,' said one.

'Let's go and find him,' said another.

'We must take gifts and go to worship him,' said a third.

The wise men set off on a long journey, following the star.

They stopped in Jerusalem, but King Herod could tell them nothing about the baby king. Then they followed the star to Bethlehem where they found Mary with her child. They gave him their gifts of gold, frankincense and myrrh, and worshipped him.

# JESUS THE TEACHER



**W**hen Mary's son was grown up, he chose twelve men to be his special friends. Then he started to teach the people all he knew about God and about the best way for people to live their lives.

'The people who are happy are those who know how much they need God's help and forgiveness,' Jesus said.

'If someone hurts you, be kind to them. Go out of your way to help everyone, even your enemies. It's easy to love people who already love us. God wants us to be different.

'Learn to love God more than the things you own. Love other people more than money. One day moths or rust will

destroy your belongings. Make sure you have
stored treasure in heaven where nothing can destroy it.

'Don't worry about what you will eat or drink, or what
clothes you have. God makes sure the birds have enough to eat.
God makes the flowers in the fields beautiful. God cares even
more about you.

'Put God first in your life, and he will make sure that you
have everything you need – and much more besides.'

# THE STORM ON THE LAKE



It was the end of a long day. Jesus climbed into a boat to sail across Lake Galilee with his friends. They had not sailed far when Jesus fell asleep, rocked by the motion of the boat.

Then the wind began to blow harder. Rain clouds moved quickly across the sky. The sails flapped. The waves crashed against the sides of the boat and tossed it high in the water.

Jesus' friends clung to the mast. They tried to wake Jesus.

'Help us!' they shouted over the noise of the wind. 'We're going to drown!'

Jesus stood up.

'Be quiet!' he shouted to the wind. 'Be still!' he shouted to the waves. The wind stopped howling. The sea grew calm again.

The men in the boat were amazed. Jesus had power over the wind and the waves. He spoke – and they obeyed him.

# THE HUNGRY CROWD

*Matthew 14:13-21*

Jesus told the people about how much God loved them.
Jesus healed people who were ill: after they had been with
Jesus, the blind could see, the deaf could hear, the lame
could walk. So when Jesus went into the countryside, a
large crowd of people followed him.

When evening came, Jesus knew that everyone was hungry.
'Where can we buy food for these people?' Jesus asked his
friend, Philip.

'For all these people?' Philip asked, amazed. 'It would
cost far too much money!'

Just then, Andrew, another of Jesus'
friends, came to him.

'This little boy has five small barley
rolls and two little fish,' he said.

Jesus smiled at the boy and took the
food in his hands. 'Tell everyone to sit
down,' Jesus said.

Jesus thanked God for the food,
broke the bread and the fish and shared
it with his friends. His friends shared
the bread and fish with the people sitting
on the grass. Everyone began to eat.

There was enough for all the people there,
and his friends collected twelve baskets full of
what was left over. More than five thousand
people had been fed that day by Jesus. It was a
miracle.

# The good Samaritan

*Luke 10:25-37*

One day, a man came to Jesus and asked him how he could please God.

'Love God and love your neighbour,' Jesus replied.

'But who is my neighbour?' asked the man. Jesus told the man a story.

'A man was travelling from Jerusalem to Jericho when he was attacked by robbers and left for dead.

'A priest came that way but pretended not to see him. Another holy man came and saw the man too, but

he went on his journey without stopping. Finally, a man from another country came along. He went to help straight away. He cleaned his wounds, put him on his own donkey and took him to an inn, where he paid the innkeeper to look after him till he was well.'

Jesus turned to the man. 'Who do you think was a good neighbour to the injured man?'

'The one who helped him,' he said.

Jesus said, 'That's the way to please God.'

# Jesus Heals a Blind Man



Bartimaeus could not see. Day by day, he sat by the side of the road and held out his begging bowl as the people walked by.

One day, Bartimaeus heard many voices, laughing and chattering, the sound of a huge crowd of people approaching.

'Who is there?' shouted Bartimaeus. 'Tell me, what's happening?'

'Jesus is coming!' someone answered him.

Bartimaeus knew all about Jesus. Jesus talked to people about God. Jesus performed miracles…

'Jesus! Help me!' shouted Bartimaeus over the sound of the crowd.

'Be quiet!' someone answered.

'Stop shouting!' said someone else.

But Jesus had heard Bartimaeus.

'Tell him to come here,' Jesus said.

'Jesus is asking for you,' said a kind voice. Bartimaeus threw off his cloak and scrambled to his feet. He put out his arms and felt his way through the crowd.

'What do you want me to do for you?' asked Jesus.

'I want to see!' said Bartimaeus.

'You believe that I can help you,' smiled Jesus. 'Go! You can see.'

Bartimaeus opened his eyes. He found he could see the faces of all the people around him. He could see the bright sunlight. He could see Jesus smiling at him. He had been healed!

Jesus turned to go on his way. Bartimaeus joined the crowd and followed Jesus.

# THE LITTLE TAX COLLECTOR

*Luke 19:1-10*

Zacchaeus was a tax collector and a cheat. But he wanted very much to meet Jesus.

Zacchaeus stood at the back of the crowd lining the street in Jericho, but because he was not very tall, he could see nothing but the backs of everyone's heads, and because he had no friends, no one would let him through.

So Zacchaeus climbed into the branches of a fig tree. He saw Jesus walking along the road. He saw Jesus look up into the branches of the tree…

'Hello, Zacchaeus! Why don't you come down so I can come to your house today?' Jesus said.

Zaccheaus scrambled
down the tree. Jesus wanted to
be his friend!

'I'm sorry I have taken more money
than I should have,' Zacchaeus said. 'I want to
give lots of my money to the poor, and I will give back to
anyone I have cheated even more than I owe them!'

Jesus smiled. Zacchaeus would never be the same again.

# THE LAST MEAL

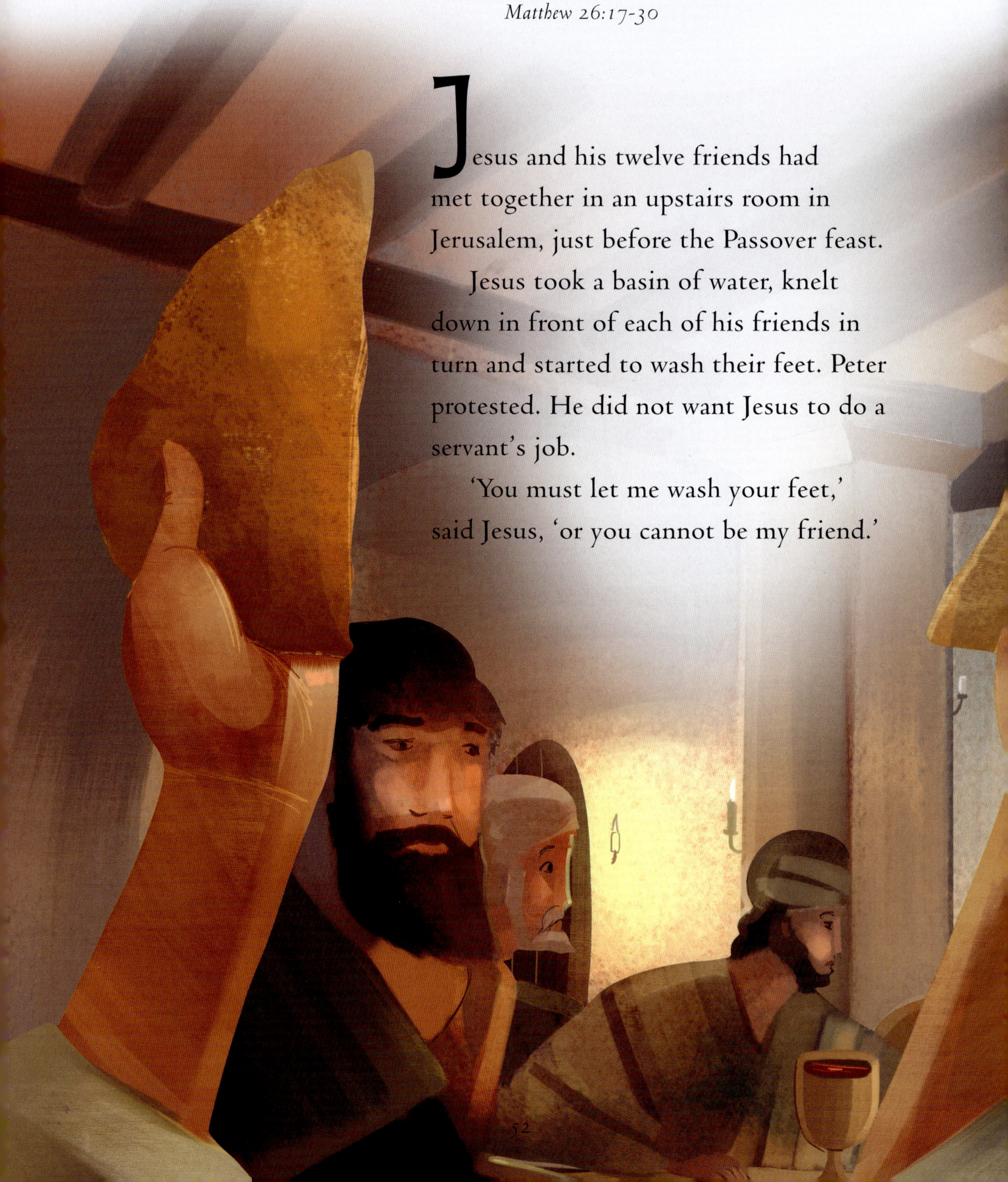

Jesus and his twelve friends had met together in an upstairs room in Jerusalem, just before the Passover feast.

Jesus took a basin of water, knelt down in front of each of his friends in turn and started to wash their feet. Peter protested. He did not want Jesus to do a servant's job.

'You must let me wash your feet,' said Jesus, 'or you cannot be my friend.'

'Then wash my hands and head as well!' said
Peter.

'There's no need,' said Jesus. 'I am
showing you how you must serve one
another. You must not be afraid to follow
my example. Then others will know that
you are different — you care about each
other.'

As they ate, Jesus told his friends that
this would be their last meal together.
He had made enemies among the
religious leaders; soon he would be
betrayed by one of his friends; soon
he would die. Then Judas left the room
and went out into the night.

Jesus thanked God for the bread and
broke it into pieces.

'This is my body, which is given for
you,' he said. 'Remember me whenever you
eat together like this.' Then Jesus picked up
a cup of red wine. 'This is my blood, shed for
you, so that your sins can be forgiven.'

Jesus' friends ate and drank with
him, but they did not understand what
he was telling them.

FRIENDS RUN AWAY
Mark 14:43-50

Jesus took his disciples to an olive garden called Gethsemane.

'Wait here while I pray,' he said to them.

Peter, James and John went with him a little further, then they also stopped.

Jesus walked away so he could be alone.

'Father God, I want to do all that you ask of me. But if it's possible to save me from the death that lies ahead of me, please help me now.'

Jesus went back to Peter, James and John. They had fallen asleep.

'Could you not even stay awake with me for a little while?' Jesus asked.

They all looked up as they heard the sounds of a crowd coming through the garden. Judas walked up to Jesus and kissed him. It was the signal for the men to rush forward and arrest Jesus. Judas had betrayed Jesus. They marched him away to the house of Caiaphas, the High Priest, so that they could put him on trial. But his other friends ran away and left him.

Jesus was passed from the High Priest to Pontius Pilate, the Roman governor. Jesus had committed no sin; they could find no crime to accuse him of.

# DEATH ON A CROSS

*Mark 15:8-20*

A crowd waited outside to hear
what Pontius Pilate would do. But
Jesus' enemies had made sure the
crowd was full of their supporters.
When Pilate asked the crowd what
he should do with Jesus, they
cried, 'Crucify him! Crucify him!'

So Pilate let the soldiers take
Jesus away.

They dressed him up in a
purple robe and put a crown of
thorns on his head. Then they
beat him and spat in his face.

They took him away
to the place of execution
outside the city walls and
crucified him between two
thieves.



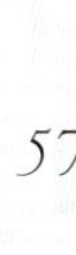

# THE
# EMPTY TOMB

*Matthew 28:1-10*

Jesus died on the cross. He was taken down before the Sabbath started and was buried in a tomb. A large stone was rolled in front to seal the entrance.

Early on the Sunday morning, two women, some of Jesus' friends, went to the tomb. They had brought oils and spices so they could anoint his body properly. But when they got there, they saw that someone had rolled the huge stone away from the entrance. The tomb was empty.

Then an angel spoke to the women.

'I know you are looking for Jesus,' the angel said, 'but he is not here. God has raised him from death, just as he told you. Come and look for yourself – then tell all his friends that he is alive!'

The women were both afraid and overjoyed at the news. Then, as they went from the garden, they met Jesus and fell at his feet, worshipping him.

'Don't be afraid,' Jesus said. 'Go and tell my friends that I am alive and I will see them soon.'

The women ran with the news.

'Jesus is alive! We have seen him with our own eyes!'

Jesus appeared again. His friends knew that he really had risen from the dead. But Thomas had not been there.

'Unless I see him myself, I cannot believe it!' said Thomas.

The friends met together now only behind locked doors. Suddenly Jesus appeared.

'Peace be with you,' he greeted them. 'Thomas, come here. Put your fingers in the nail marks. Feel for yourself the place in my side where they put the spear. Believe that I am alive!'

'My Lord and my God!' Thomas said, falling to his knees.

Jesus ate and talked with his friends many more times before he went back to be with God in heaven. Then he sent them the Holy Spirit, so they had power to tell everyone they knew that God loved them and wanted them all to be his friends.